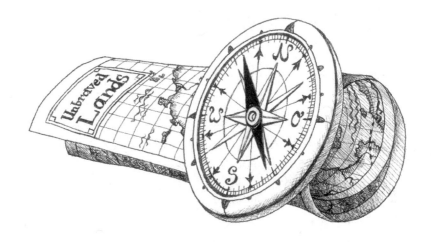

# Impressum

**Managing Editor:**

Till Bay
Comerge AG
Bubenbergstrasse 1
8045 Zurich
Switzerland

Tel: +41 43 501 38 38
Fax: +41 43 501 38 39

Email: till.bay@comerge.net

**Associate Editors:**

Benno Baumgartner
Matthias Hüni
Eva Jutzeler
Michela Pedroni

**Layout and Artwork:**

Eva Jutzeler

all rights reserved © July 2014 by Comerge AG, Switzerland

**Publisher:**

buch & netz, Zürich
http://buchundnetz.com

This book is available as print or ebook:

ISBN 978-3-03805-035-3 (Print)
ISBN 978-3-03805-101-5 (PDF)
ISBN 978-3-03805-102-2 (ePub)
ISBN 978-3-03805-103-9 (mobi)

# Co-Pilot

## using agile methods to land IT projects smoothly

# Preface to the first edition

There are many books on agile methods and software development best practices available today. So why write another book on the topic?

There are a number of reasons: First of all, we do not believe in taking a book and following it word for word. We rather trust in action and daily practice. The book you are holding in your hands describes a set of process patterns that have worked well for us in the past. By constantly remixing and improving them, we ensure that they continue to fit the needs of our evolving company. In fact, the Co-Pilot includes a framework for adapting the process to changes, thus driving it further as we write. Hence, this book does not describe a specific menu to cook in the software kitchen, but it describes a list of ingredients and spices that can be mixed and matched.

The second reason for turning our practices into written form is: the ideas described in the Co-Pilot may be reused by other companies in other environments applying a similar mix and match approach. The way of working defines and significantly influences a company's culture, but it can only become culture if you are convinced of the practices. We hope that the processes and methods described in the Co-Pilot will entice you to choose some and invent your own flavor of an agile software development process to be implemented at your company. The name of this book—Co-Pilot—reflects this idea. It serves as guidance and inspiration and provides inputs, but you remain the pilot in charge.

The processes and ideas that the Co-Pilot describes have roots in the history of our company, Comerge. Comerge grew in its first ten months from four employees to over twenty. During this rapid evolution, we were confronted with various managerial and technological challenges.

Coming to a slower growth pace in recent months (we are now almost three years old) motivated us to look back and identify the ideas that helped us master these challenges while still satisfying the needs of our customers. Many of these ideas have their roots in our experience as employees or co-workers of inspiring proponents of agile software methods: Benno Baumgartner and Till Bay have worked at Erich Gamma's lab, five of us worked for Bertrand Meyer at the Chair of Software Engineering at ETH Zurich, and others have managed outsourcing projects with programmers located in Eastern Europe. The Co-Pilot collects these experiences and the best practices of our past and present.

We hope that you enjoy the read and that it inspires you to put some of it into action at your company.

We would like to thank the following people for making this book possible: Daniela Bomatter, Julian Tschannen, Geraldine von Roten, and Urs Doenni for their reviews of the drafts, Eva Jutzeler for her fantastic layout and drawings, and all our customers and employees for their constant support and encouragement. You are great and together we make the shipping of high quality software happen and safely land agile software projects.


November 2010

Till Bay

# Preface to the second edition

A lot has happened since the first edition of the Co-Pilot came out in November 2010: Comerge has celebrated its sixth birthday and looking back at the last four years, Comerge has undergone an evolution in various areas.

First of all, we are happy to have gained many new talented and motivated Comergers as colleagues. This has meant for us that new ideas, expectations, and needs have entered our company life and helped shape what Comerge is today. At the same time, company growth has put us up against managerial and organizational challenges, which the Co-Pilot has helped us handle. These new challenges have also lead to changes in the Co-Pilot that—where needed—we have adapted to fit our needs.

Secondly, we are proud of the going live of several large projects (the most prominent being the Mobility project, live since October 2011). Having safely landed these software projects has affirmed the value of the Co-Pilot and strengthens our belief in following its processes while continuously advancing its principles as the company, the team, and our projects evolve.

Thirdly, we have moved the tool support for the Co-Pilot process from Origo to JIRA and have started using Git instead of Subversion (SVN) for our projects. These technological changes have rendered some of the contents of the Co-Pilot's first edition outdated and resulted in adaptations to the process descriptions and extensions detailing the peculiarities of these tools.

All of these developments have effects on how we work and to stay abreast of changes, it is high time to bring out a second edition of the Co-Pilot! We hope you will find the Co-Pilot interesting and helpful.

We would like to thank all our customers and colleagues for their loyalty, trust and commitment to jointly developing high quality software. Special thanks go to Benno Baumgartner who contributed many inputs for the way we work and to Patrick Ferrarelli for his insights on book typesetting that have found their way into this second edition.

Enjoy the read and let us know how the Co-Pilot is used in your team!

July 2014

Till Bay

# Table of contents

# Tests

# Customers

# Our values

Growing revenue and cutting down on costs is a key topic for successful businesses and corporate goals are often stated in financial terms. But goals that are purely focused on gains may lead to opportunistic and unethical behavior. Recent newspapers are full of examples—insider trading, bribery, invasion of privacy—just to name a few. In some cases, this even results in the downfall of employees or the entire company.

## Create a business we can be proud of

Comerge is as interested in making profit as any other company. But our vision is also to be able to look back 20 years from now and feel pride for the company that we helped shape. We want to stand behind the ethical principles it represents and the actions that we have taken throughout the company's history.

This is where our values come in. They govern our strategies and help us make the right decisions when short-term profit or other pressures entice us to take a wrong path. Our values represent our core ideologies and are non-negotiable principles.

We have captured our views in five statements, each reflecting who we are, how we do business, and what we want to focus on.

# The Comerge Values

## Be curious

We founded Comerge, because we wanted to know what it means to have a company. Not much has changed. We chase every opportunity to learn something new – wherever we go and whomever we talk to. We are interested in ideas and views of others: when we speak to our customers, to users, to colleagues at work, or to our friends. We are creative and challenge the status quo. We are curious, but we never loose track of the goals.

## Be commercial

We are a commercial business. Hence, creating growth and profit for us and our customers is central. We need to be tough, but at the same time fair. We think clearly, act decisively, and never loose track of the top priorities. We are commercial, but we are also ethical.

## Be responsible

We know what the right thing to do is and we do it. We are conscious of the consequences of our actions, in both the short and the long term. We try to leave things a little better than we find them, and we encourage others to join us in this endeavor. We appreciate if our colleagues go ahead and take responsibility for what they do and we try to follow suit and be equally proactive in our daily decisions.

## Be engineering

We want to do what we do better than anyone else, and have fun doing it. And what we do best is engineering. People count on our software and they trust us to build the best software possible. We do that because we are engineers at heart. We do not build half-baked software.

## Be evolving

With our feedback to others, with our work guided by our values, by simply living on this planet, we constantly see change. We value responding to change more than following a plan. Things never stay what they are and by embracing change and evolving together with the world around us, we create a competitive advantage for our customers and a more exciting life for ourselves.

# How to read

This book describes an agile software development process. It relies on three cornerstones: the key process roles, a specific iteration setup, and the notion of issues. The *process roles* define the hierarchical structure of stakeholders within a project. They also determine the duties that the stakeholders have during a project and how they interact. The duties of stakeholders result in tasks that they work on, which in the end will lead to a software product. These tasks are captured in *issues*. The *iteration setup* controls when and how issues are handled. Every project is based on a sequence of iterations with a fixed length (usually 5 weeks). At the end of each iteration (the milestone), the development team provides a release to the customer.

The rest of this book shows how these notions can be put to practice and describes processes to successfully land a software project with the help of the Co-Pilot. To help navigate through the different chapters, we have divided the book into four parts:

- **Projects:** This part describes all the processes revolving around the planning of projects, handling of issues, and organization of iterations. It also provides more detailed information on how issues should be reviewed, how we use the branching infrastructure of Git to support this task, and what we expect from our employees concerning the tracking of their time.

- **Meetings:** Following the processes of the Co-Pilot, several meetings regularly take place during an iteration (e.g., the retrospective meeting or the daily Scrum meeting). The *Meetings* part of the Co-Pilot details on the setup and agenda of these meetings.

- **Testing:** Testing is a crucial activity when targeting the goal of delivering high quality software. Thus, the various testing practices are shown in this part of the book.

– **Customers:** Agile software development entails a high degree of involvement of the customer. This part of the book describes best practices when collaborating with customers and shows how to provide support services to customers after a product has gone live.

## Notes to the reader

Many of the terms used in this book have very specific meanings in the context of the process framework that the Co-Pilot describes. The glossary at the end of the book provides definitions of the terms and we ask you to refer to it.

The book uses "he" and "she" interchangeably. Both pronouns always mean to include males and females. To make reading easier, we consistently used the female pronoun for certain process roles and the male pronoun for others.

# Projects

# Process roles

Our software development process is based on the four roles: team member, team lead, product manager, and customer.

## Team member

The main activity of a team member is to resolve issues. Issues capture things to do. They are sufficiently small grained to be solved in a short time frame (usually taking at most one day). Issues result from bug reports or enhancement wishes. Every issue can be assigned to a specific team member, who then is responsible for resolving it (see **How to work with issues** for more information on issues). The team members of a company may have any professional background (e.g., designers, marketing agents, assistants, education specialists), but in a software company most of them will probably be software engineers. A software developing team member owns a clearly defined portion of the code. As a code owner, she is responsible for her code and expected to be the expert.

## Team lead

The team lead communicates with other teams and the product manager. He is responsible for assigning issues to his team members and for planning an iteration. The team lead should always know what his team members are working on and when they will be finished. He may redistribute work among them and thus balance the workload evenly. It is the team lead's responsibility that his team achieves the goals of an iteration. The team lead reports the status (green, yellow, red) of the iteration during the weekly core meeting. The team lead is also a team member.

## Product manager

The product manager is responsible for the entire product. She gathers the requirements from the customer and communicates these requirements to the team leads by using user stories and enhancements. She makes sure that the teams implement the enhancements as expected. Her goal is to find out how to satisfy the needs of the customer while taking into account the resources of the teams. The product manager keeps an overview of all teams and directs their work towards one common goal. Ideally, the product manager is a business manager with a technical background, and sometimes, she is an employee of the customer.

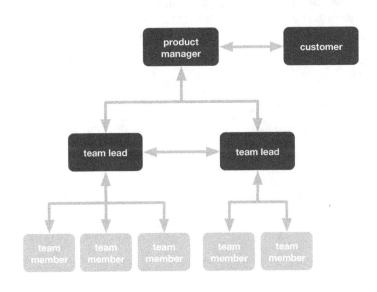

## Customer

One important goal of the process is to satisfy the customer. In return, the customer pays the bill. Usually, there is one person appointed as customer representative. This person is an employee of the customer and has two main duties:

1.   He continuously observes the progress of the product development and ensures that it is on track.

2.   He protects the project teams against internal customer politics and acts as a channel to communicate customer decisions.

If the customer representative is not willing or not capable of fulfilling both duties, the product manager tries to fill the gap and supports the customer representative. If this fails, the product development may be carried out, but it is unlikely that the Co-Pilot will be able to deliver a product that matches the needs of the customer. Another process or customer should be considered in this case.

# How to plan a project

A project is an endeavor undertaken to bring an idea to life by creating a unique product. In such a setting, changes happen frequently – thus, it is important to identify and plan the fundamentals of the project that remain stable.

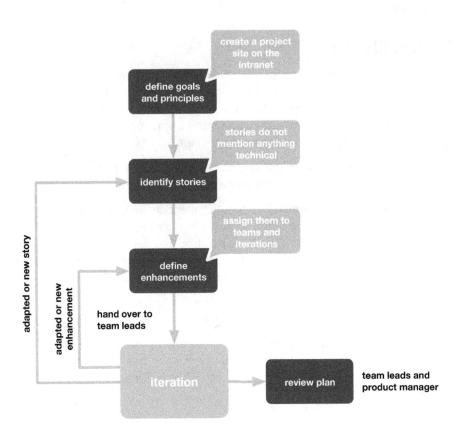

# Define goals and principles

What is the goal of your project? The product manager creates a project workspace on the Intranet and uses it to:

- Clarify the focus. This leads to stories.

- Document the resources (people, software, hardware, books, etc.) that are needed.

- Define success.

- Clarify principles or constraints. For example: Is the main goal to please the boss, stay within budget, or finish by a certain deadline?

# Identify stories

Stories are simple descriptions of what the software should accomplish. These stories are developed by the customer and the developing team. Given a story, the team members create issues. This is an open process; finding the stories may rely on any useful technique like brainstorming or mind maps.

**Note:** Stories do not mention technical details. The gathering of stories usually happens at the beginning of every iteration.

- **Define enhancements:** The product manager breaks down the stories into enhancements, documents them as issues, and assigns them to teams and iterations. She also provides priorities and a rough chronological order for the enhancements. She then hands the iteration planning over to the team leads.

- **Iteration:** The teams carry out an iteration (see also How to iterate). This may lead to adapted or new enhancements and stories.

- **Review the iteration plan:** After each iteration, the team leads and the product manager gather to review it. This review discusses if the goals of the iteration were fulfilled. This review can be done as part of the retrospective meeting.

## Assigning team members

Generally, it is a bad idea to assign a team member to work on two projects at the same time in one iteration, because it requires a lot of discipline from the team member.

While it is possible to divide a week into two parts, each devoted to working on one project, work is in reality often fragmented. Fragmentation appears when the times in which the person needs to be in one place overlap with times where the person needs to be somewhere else. If it cannot be avoided (typically the case in startups where all employees share the workload and help each other), it requires very clear planning of the person's resources.

# Example

This example shows a user story and related enhancements. The overall goal is to develop a software that manages the customers of a company.

## User story

**Title:** Opening a customer by customer ID

**Description:** As a call center agent, I want to open a customer by entering his customer ID, so that I can quickly access his data when he is calling the call center and identifying himself with his customer ID.

## Enhancement for the frontend team

The web user interface allows quick navigation to a customer profile by entering the customer ID.

**Task:** Implement a number field that allows to enter a customer ID on all the pages of the software. Hitting the button

"Go!" or the "enter" key opens the customer's profile, if available. If the profile is not available, show a message stating that the customer does not exist.

## Enhancement for the backend team

We need a way to construct a URL to show the profile of a customer given his customer ID.

**Task:** Implement the getCustomerUrl service, which constructs a URL given a customer ID or returns an error message if the customer does not exist.

# How to iterate

An iteration is one cycle in the release process. Usually an iteration is 5 weeks long and has three phases:

- **Planning:** 2–3 days

- **Implementing:** ~4 weeks

- **Testing:** 1 week (see How to create a release for details).

The exact duration is up to the taste of the team. 5 weeks works for us, but we also heard from other teams that a shorter duration is practicable. We prefer our iterations to always have the same lengths, to ensure that the team is aware of it and embraces the rythm.

## In the planning phase ...

... the team lead assigns the enhancements that were defined in the project planning to the team members. Additionally, the team lead also distributes tasks and issues to team members. Tasks are parts of an enhancement and can be used to break down an enhancement into a number of smaller pieces of work. Issues come from testing the software and from user feedback. In the planning phase, the team lead also assigns issues that were postponed from previous iterations to team members.

## In the implementation phase ...

... all team members work on their enhancements, issues, and bugs. During this phase, no requests from outside of the team should be accepted (read below on how to handle asynchronous requests).

During the core meeting, the team members report on their progress of the projects they are working on.

## In the testing phase ...

... the software development is first frozen and then tested according to a test plan. See How to create a release for details. After creating the release the iteration is over and it is time to take a nice break, read a book, plant a tree, or have a BBQ.

## Asynchronous requests

*A customer or product manager approaches a team member with an asynchronous request in the middle of an iteration.*

Generally this is not allowed. And thus, it is important that the product manager explains this rule (and the general process) to the customer at the beginning of the project, so that they understand why a request is pushed back. A team member that faces an asynchronous request may handle it in the following way:

– If it is the product manager that approaches a team member, then the team member may tell her to improve the planning next time and refuse to accept the request.

– If it is the customer, then the product manager explains to him that it is not practical for the success and quality of the current iteration.

If the request is critical and comes in before the freeze of the iteration's milestone, the product manager may offer to trade the new enhancement against one of the enhancements that was planned for the iteration.

# How to work with issues

Issues are one of the core concepts of the Co-Pilot. There are several rules to follow when dealing with issues:

- Every code change is caused by an issue.

- Every request for a code change must be filed as an issue.

- An issue can only be resolved as fixed, if it has an assignee and fix version.

It is important to track issues because of the following reasons:

- Issues can be viewed as a list of things that a team member needs to do. Filing an issue ensures that the "to do" is not forgotten.

- Issues may be assigned to a person. Once an issue is assigned, it is clear who is its owner and thus responsible to resolve it.

- It is often difficult to understand somebody else's code changes and why a change has been done. An issue describing it, even just briefly, helps a lot.

- Issues help track changes. An issue can be reopened, reassigned, prioritized, it can be used for discussions, and it supports planning.

- Issues help stakeholders who do not look at the committed code stay informed on the project's progress and supported functionality.

- Issues visualize what, when, and by whom changes occur. This, for example, allows testers to verify fixes.

The main goal of issues is to enable all involved parties to track the work performed by the team members. As a consequence of this transparent setup, team members take responsibility for their work. This is not used to blame them for any mistakes, but it helps to make problems and miscommunication visible while there is still time to react. Additionally, team members may learn from the mistakes of others.

# Issue states

## Status

At any moment in its lifetime, an issue has exactly one status. During the lifetime of an issue, several status changes may occur. The Co-Pilot defines following statuses:

**Open:** An open issue is part of an inbox that will be checked periodically by the team lead.

**Triaged:** This is an issue that has undergone the scrutiny of a team lead and is planned in a milestone or becomes part of the backlog.

**Resolved:** An issue with a resolution tag. A resolved issue is no longer considered an issue in the product. Several different resolutions exist: See *Resolutions* below for details.

**Reviewed:** If an issue needs to be reviewed, its status should be set to reviewing and the name of the team member who must review the issue should be included. Once the reviewer has successfully reviewed the issue, the reviewer should set the status of the issue to reviewed. See How to create a release for details about the reviewing process.

**Verified:** If an issue needs to be verified, its status should be set to verification and a team member should be appointed to verify the issue. Once the verifier has successfully verified the issue, the verifier status should be changed to verifiied. See How to create a release for details on the verification process.

**Closed:** A resolved issue can be marked as closed. A closed issue must not and can not be verified.

## Resolutions

When setting an issue's state to resolved, the assignee must provide a reason, the so-called resolution. There are the following resolutions:

**Fixed:** This means that the issue is fixed.

**Won't fix:** Sometimes it does not make sense to fix an issue. Either because it has already been fixed or because it is irrelevant. A comment to explain why an issue will not be fixed is mandatory.

**Works for me:** In some cases an issues cannot be reproduced by the programmer. In this case the issues should be closed as works for me.

**Duplicate:** Sometimes the same or similar issues are created more than once. In this case the newer issues or those that are less descriptive can be closed as duplicate.

**Verified:** When an issue has gone through the verification process, then its resolution will be verified indicating that an additional person has checked that the issue is fixed.

## Assignee

The assignee of an issue is responsible for the issue to be resolved. Only issues that have an assignee can and will be resolved. It is common that the assignee of an issue is determined on the fly during iterations or at the beginning of each iteration during the iteration planning. Larger projects with multiple teams use the "component" tag to assign issue responsibilities to a specific team.

## Affected Version

The affected version specifies the version of the product in which the issue was detected. This information is crucial to reproduce the issue.

## Fix version

Each issue should have a fix version. If the issue is still open, the fix version determines in which iteration it must be resolved. If it is fixed or verified, it describes in which iteration the issue was resolved. It is common that the fix version of an issue changes. This might happen if an issue must be postponed to a later iteration

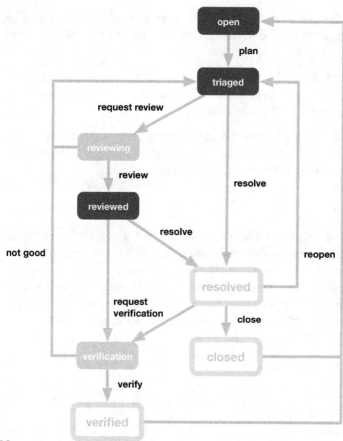

because of lack of time or an impediment (a required other issue) that could not be resolved on time, or if the project progress allows to resolve an issue earlier than initially planned. It is also common practice to set the fix version on the fly during an iteration. To re-solve an issue, the fix version must be set.

# Example

The following example describes a typical life cycle for an issue. When creating a new issue, the following information must be entered:

- the project it belongs to

- if available, the component it is associated to (this deter-mines the responsible team, if there are multiple teams in a project)

- an affected version, so that the issue can be reproduced

- an issue description stating the problem in such a way that another person can reproduce the error or understand what needs to be done for a new feature

After the creation of the issue, it will be in status "Open".

The team leads regularly check their component's inbox and triage the issues by setting their status to "Triaged", assigning them to a team member, and determining their "Fix version". Before the team member commits a fix, she may request a review by another team member by setting the status of the issue to "Reviewing". After having the OK from the reviewer, the issue may also need to be verified by setting its status to "Verification".

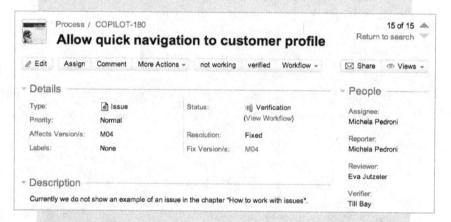

Once the issue has been verified, its status and resolution will be "Verified".

# Priorities

An issue may have a priority. The higher the priority the faster the issue should be resolved. A critical or blocker issue has always high priority and a minor one has always a low priority. The Co-Pilot defines the following priorities:

**Blocker:** The product cannot be used without this issue being resolved. It blocks development and/or testing. The assigned team member should immediately start fixing this issue.

**Major or Critical:** The issue is a must do and needs to be done first. It is very hard to use the product with this issue. It is unacceptable to have such an issue in a release.

**Normal:** It is a normal bug. It should be fixed if possible. Do this after all issues with higher priority have been fixed. Issues with normal priorities are generally expected to be resolved in the product.

**Minor or Trivial:** A small bug which might even stay unrecognized by most users. Do this after all issues with higher priority have been resolved. Issues with low priorities are usually nice to have. It is only acceptable to fix such an issue if the risk of introducing a new, more severe bug, is low. It is no problem to release the product leaving these issues unresolved.

# Examples

**Blocker:** It is not possible to log in.

**Critical:** Product crashes, data is lost, or security does not withstand attack.

**Major:** Display flickers, refresh sometimes does not reload.

**Normal:** A commonly expected keyboard shortcut does not work, e.g. hitting the "enter" key in a text box for quick opening a customer profile is not working.

**Minor:** Border is 2 pixel too far to the left in Internet Explorer 7.

# How to triage issues

Change is the only constant in a project. Thus, triaging issues is a continuous process. Whenever a new issue comes in, the triaging should happen within the next 24 hours to ensure that the project and the team members stay on top of things. While triaging issues, they learn how their customers use the product and notice the difficult spots immediately. Hence, triaging issues is all about communication.

## Take an issue from the inbox

An unassigned, unowned issue without a target first appears in the inbox of the inbox triager. Usually, the product manager takes the role of inbox triager. He distributes the issues to the teams. The team leads of the components then process the issues in their components' inbox and assign them to their team members and decide on a target. If a team member reports an issue that is rooted in her owned code, she may circumvent this process and directly assign it to herself. Generally, all parties should constantly keep track of the inbox and their issue states, at a minimum on a daily basis.

## Reproduce the issue

To understand an issue it needs to be reproduced. The reproduction should happen shortly after the first issue report, because it may require contacting the reporter to clarify any uncertainties. The reproduction may result in three possible outcomes:

- The issue can be reproduced.

- The issue cannot be reproduced.

- It is unclear how to reproduce the issue.

There is a thin line between cannot and do not know how to reproduce. If the person working on the issue is not able to reproduce the issue, she can always request details from the reporter to better understand what he did.

# Handling reproducible issues

Issues that can be reproduced will most likely be resolved as "duplicate", "won't fix", "fixed", or "verified".

## Close as duplicate or won't fix

An issue is resolved as "duplicate", if it can be reproduced and is already captured by another issue. The reporter must be notified about the existing issue by adding a comment, such as "duplicate of issue #1234", when closing the issue. If the issue can be reproduced and is resolved as "won't fix", it will not be fixed. The issue description needs to contain a good, comprehensible reason for not fixing it. Not giving a reason violates the netiquette.

## Close as fixed or verified

If the issue is understood and it has been decided to fix it, then the issue is planned and/or assigned. It is required to either assign the issue to a team member or plan the issue for an iteration or both. It is also desirable to set the severity and priority in this step. See "How to work with issues" for a definition of all the severity and priority levels.

Fixing an issue involves several additional steps:

- **Fix the issue:** Fixing the issue will result in a code change, thus it should be accompanied by a unit test (if possible). This ensures that the issue will not reappear in future releases.

- **Reviewing fix:** It may also be required that the code change is reviewed by another person before the issue can be closed as fixed. This is optional. See How to create a release for details about the reviewing process.

- **Close as fixed:** After the fixing, the issue resolution is set to "fixed". A comment accompanies the issue and describes in which revision of the code the issue was fixed. The developer should make sure that all unit tests are green before they close the issue.

- **Verify fix:** Before the next release takes place, the issue should be verified. This means that a person different from the owner of the issue tries to reproduce the issue. If he cannot reproduce it, the issue state is changed to "verified". Otherwise, the issue is reopened and has to be planned and fixed again.

# Irreproducible or cryptic issues

## Close as works for me

An issue may receive the resolution "works for me", if the assigned team member is sure that she understands the issue, but cannot reproduce it. The issue should contain an explanation why and how it works. As an example, she might write "This already works, see the FooBar preference page and enable X". Usually, issues with this resolution are caused by a user error.

## Request details

If the issue report contains vague or incomplete information and thus makes it impossible to reproduce the issue, the reporter should provide more information. As an example, he might need to provide the specific system (operating system, browser, programming language version) that he worked with. If the reporter does not react or fails to provide any information that makes the issue reproducible, the team member may decide to close the issue as "works for me". Of course, it is not desirable to close an issue that is not fully understood, so everything possible should be done to get the feedback.

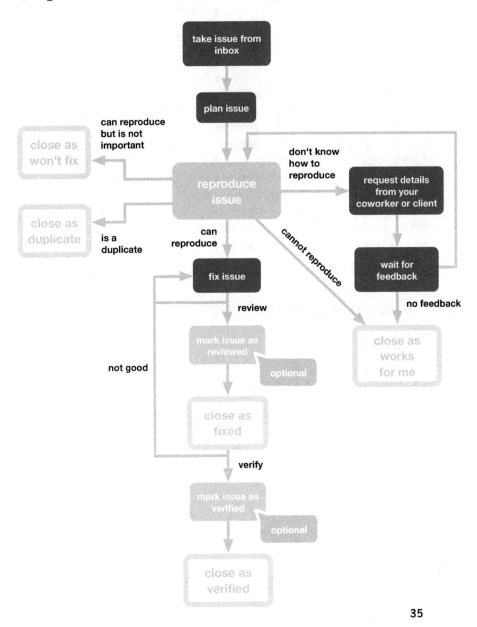

# How to plan a release week

Planning a release week involves allocating people to the freezing, testing and releasing activities so that all involved parties can complete their work and contribute optimally to making the release happen. During a test and release week, the tasks executed by team members and team leads differ from the work done during the development weeks. Thus, it is especially important to understand what needs to be done and where help is required. The planning of the test and release week is the job of the product manager, the team leads and the team members. The product manager is the person that knows about everybody's schedule and also has an overview about the schedules of other projects that might run in parallel.

## Release week activities

### All activities

**Who:** Team members
**What:** Announces any unavailabilities early on.

This will help the team leads and the product manager organize the release week.

### Testing

**Who:** Product manager
**What:** Organizes testers and announces the testing day. If appropriate, this task can also be delegated to the team lead.

Make sure that the planned testers are available on the testing day. Possible sources for testers are:

- the project team

- people from other projects

- customers that provide testers

# Fixing

**Who:** Team lead
**What:** Ensures that at least one person with the needed technological background for fixing issues is available for every component.

This is particularly important in small teams that use a technology that is not widely spread across teams. Talk to the product manager before the release week if this can not be ensured.

# Reviewing

**Who:** Team lead
**What:** Ensures that at least one other person for reviewing is available for every component.

This is particularly important in small teams that use a technology that is not widely spread across teams. Talk to the product manager before the release week if this can not be ensured.

# Deployment

**Who:** Team lead
**What:** Ensures that there is at least one person who has the technological background to deploy the release for every component.

This is particularly important in small teams that use a technology that is not widely spread across teams. Talk to the product manager before the release week if this can not be ensured.

## Releasing

**Who:** Team lead
**What:** Ensures that there is somebody available for writing the "New and Noteworthy" of his component.

Talk to the product manager before the release week if this can not be ensured.

# The release week

Stay flexible during the release week. We all know what needs to be done in a release week: write a test plan, test, fix, review, verify, write the "New and Noteworthy" and finally deploy the release. The Co-Pilot defines these activities precisely, but the amount of work they entail can vary very much between components and also between milestones. Therefore, the team members should

- talk to each other

- offer help if all tasks assigned to her have been finished

- work as a team

# How to create a release

During the development phase, the team regularly creates releases – pieces of software that combine a set of features and are fit for showing to the customer. Every milestone ends with such a release. This allows the customer to verify that the project is well on track and to find problems close to when they arise. Being able to release a working build at any given moment is also the number one success factor of an agile team. To do so, it is essential to automatize the building, quality assurance (running automated tests and tools like findbugs) and deployment process.

## Freeze day

The freeze marks the end of development in a specific milestone. After the freeze, the development code is no longer changed until after the testing day.

### Deploy the release candidate

The most important thing when creating a release is to test the system under end user conditions. This means that a build is deployed on the system (or at least an exact copy of the system) on which it will go live. In an ideal world, the release candidate will become the release without any changes. It's the team lead's responsibility that the release candidate is released.

### Write a test plan

In parallel to the deployment of the release candidate, the teams write the test plan. Usually, each team member writes a test plan for the issues she worked on during the development phase. It is important to gather input about the test items from all stakeholders that worked on the release candidate. The product manager notifies the testers in advance to ensure that they are available during the testing days. She may also invite customers on site to participate in this activity. See the test plan template at the end of this chapter.

# Testing day

## Assign test items

Instead of a Scrum meeting a team meeting is used to assign all test items to one or several testers. After the meeting, everyone in the team knows what to test and every test item has at least one tester.

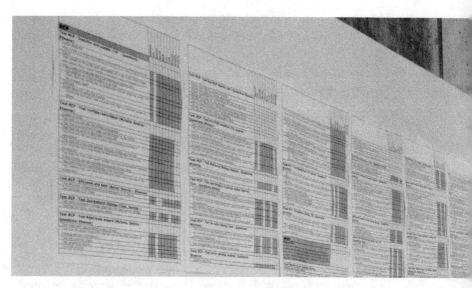

A test plan listing the test items and which testers have tested them.

### Test the release

During the testing days, the deployed release candidate is tested according to the test plan. This usually only takes one day, but in large projects it could be more. Unless a blocking issue prevents testing, no code changes are allowed during this time, because a stable baseline is needed to make sure no new issues are introduced. The testers report every failure they discover as issues in the issue tracking system. See **How to test** for details about release testing.

# Fixing days

## Issue triage meeting

After the test day each team triages all discovered issues. Triaging can be done by the team lead, a team member or in the form of a team meeting. It has been proven to be very effective if the team lead makes a first pass over the discovered issues and triages the obvious ones and then schedules a meeting with the team to discuss the remaining issues. The goal of the triaging is to identify the issues that must be fixed in order to reach an acceptable quality level for the release. It is important that the product manager defines what acceptable quality means for the current release. This highly depends on the kind of release. The acceptable quality of a milestone differs from that of a product release. The product manager may, for example, define that the release must not contain any open major issues. Usually, these quality requirements are directly derived from the contract made with the customer. Acceptable quality never means flawless. The decision what to fix and what not to fix is a very hard problem and depends on many factors. A rule of thumb is that the higher the chance that the fix for an issue will introduce a new bug the less likely it is that the issue will be fixed during the fixing days. If no more issues remain to be fixed, the release can take place. Otherwise, the teams need to fix the identified bugs, create a new release candidate, verify the fixes, and decide again if the quality is acceptable. This may, potentially, take forever, but usually requires only one or two iterations.

## Fixing and reviewing

During the fixing days, the team members fix all issues which have been planned for the current release during the issue triaging step. Each fix needs a corresponding issue. At least one review is required for each code change. The developer of the fix can choose any team member for the review. Fixes are not committed, but sent to the reviewer as a patch file (with SVN) or pushed to a branch (with Git). Issues can only be committed to the main development line after a successful review. Ideally, all the fixing and reviewing will be finished on the day before the release, so the release is not stressful. For more details about reviewing with SVN and Git, see How to review issues.

# Verifying and release day

## Deploy a new release candidate

The release candidate will be deployed again on the morning of this day under the responsibility of the team leads. It will include all fixed and reviewed issues.

## Verify fixes

All issues fixed during the fixing days are verified in the newly deployed release candidate. Verification means that a tester other than the developer who fixed the issue and other than the reviewer of the fix tries to reproduce the issue. If he cannot reproduce it, the issue is verified. Otherwise, the issue has to be reopened, fixed, reviewed and finally verified again. Every time this happens, a new release candidate has to be deployed, so the newly fixed issue can be verified. This process is repeated until the issue can be successfully verified.

## Release

Once all team leads give their approval, the release takes place. In a perfect world, the release occurs without any discernible effects to the running system. In reality, the deployment usually requires configuration steps, such as copying the release candidate to another machine or disabling access control to make a web site publicly available. After this has been done, the product manager informs all stakeholders about the release. A document containing what is new and noteworthy provides a description of new features developed in the milestone.

## Open a bottle of champagne

After the release it is important to throw a little party, have a beer together, and give the team a couple of days to relax. This is called the decompression phase.

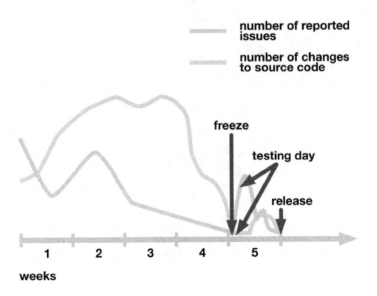

# One week later

## Retrospective meeting

In the week after the release, a retrospective meeting should be held. See **How to hold a retrospective meeting** for details.

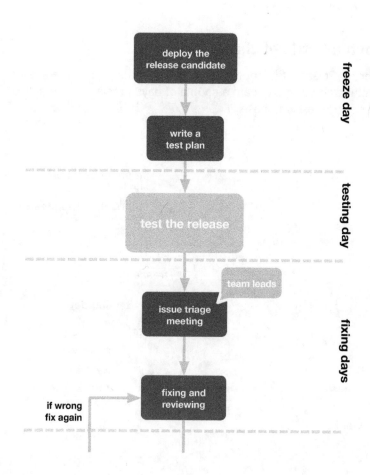

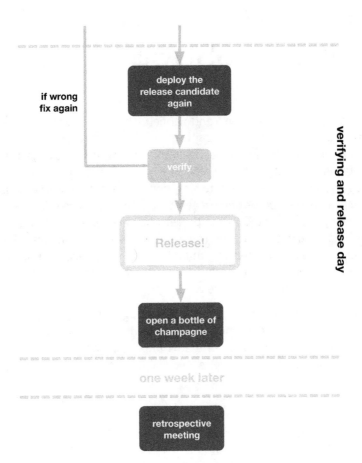

**if wrong fix again**

deploy the release candidate again

verify

Release!

open a bottle of champagne

one week later

retrospective meeting

**verifying and release day**

# How to review issues

Issues need to be reviewed and verified if they are fixed for a re-lease but are not tested during the test days of the release week. This is the case for all the issues found during the test days that are being fixed during the fix days of a release week. Since these is-sues will not go through a testing day process, the source code changes have to be peer reviewed by another team member. The reviewing step of the Co-Pilot process helps ensure that the code changes have a high quality. The verification step is done after the code changes have been committed and a new release candidate is built. It serves as a second instance of control. This chapter only describes the reviewing process.

If an issue comes in, the team lead first triages it and then assigns it to the respective team member. The team member develops a fix for the issue. The handling of the fix then depends on the version control software used for the respective project.

## SVN

The reviewing process in SVN uses patches. After a team member has produced a fix of the issue in her development environment, she will create a patch, containing all the code changes. Prefer-ably, the patch contains the issue number and project name in its filename. The patch should contain the issue number and is then attached to the issue in the issue tracker. If binary files are needed to review the issue, for example images, those have to be attached separately, as patches only work for textual files (e.g., code and configuration files). Then, a reviewer is added to the issue and the issue receives the status "reviewing". The reviewer applies the patch to her own project, checks the code and tests the fix by de-

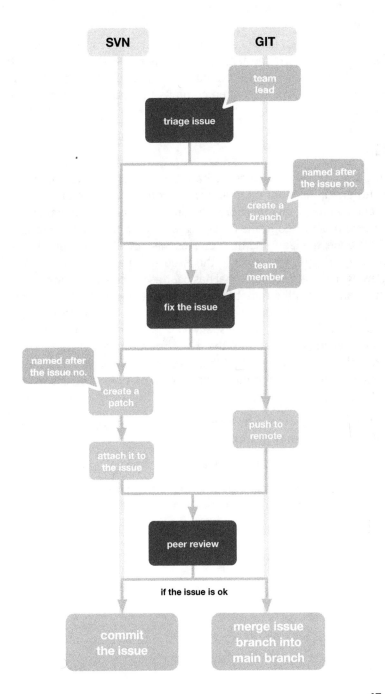

ploying the project locally and checking the changes visually. If she approves of the fix, she tags the issue as reviewed and returns it to the team member who produced the patch. After a successful review, the team member then commits the changes to the development stream.

## Git

In Git the reviewing process is based on branches. When an issue is reviewed, the team member working on the issue creates a new branch on her local repository. The branch is named containing the issue number. All code and file changes are then done on this branch. Once done, the team member pushes this branch to the remote repository, assigns a reviewer to the issue and marks the issue as reviewing. The team member that has been assigned as a reviewer pulls the branch from the remote repository, switches to the branch and reviews the code and deploys the project locally to check the changes functionally and visually. If she approves, the reviewed code branch is merged into the main branch by either the reviewer or the team member who has fixed the issue and the issue is tagged as reviewed. For more information on how to do branching with Git, see **How to use Git**.

It is also possible that a reviewer may reject an issue. This can happen on the following grounds:

- the code or other files of the patch are faulty
- the refactoring is too large and has unforeseen implications on the project that cannot be tested
- the team lead does not agree with the fix

# How to use Git

Git is a distributed version control system and at Comerge, we use it for several projects. One of the powers of Git is its flexibility in branching. The downside of this power is the danger of introducing chaos into a repository. The Co-Pilot suggests a lightweight yet flexible branching model to get the most out of Git without having to correct branching and merging mistakes frequently. This Git branching model is highly influenced by the blog post of Vincent Driessen.

For each project, one or more central Git repositories exist. This central repository is hosted on a repository server and is called *origin*. The continuous integration infrastructure and deployment process always work with this central repository.

Each developer has her own copy (i.e., clone) of the repository locally on her computer. It is up to the developer that she keeps her local repository in sync with *origin*. That is, she pushes her changes to origin when she has working commits and pulls latest changes from other developers.

● commits to the development branch

● features or bugs before the freeze or between milestones

● features or bugs after the freeze

● commits to the master branch

*Projects*

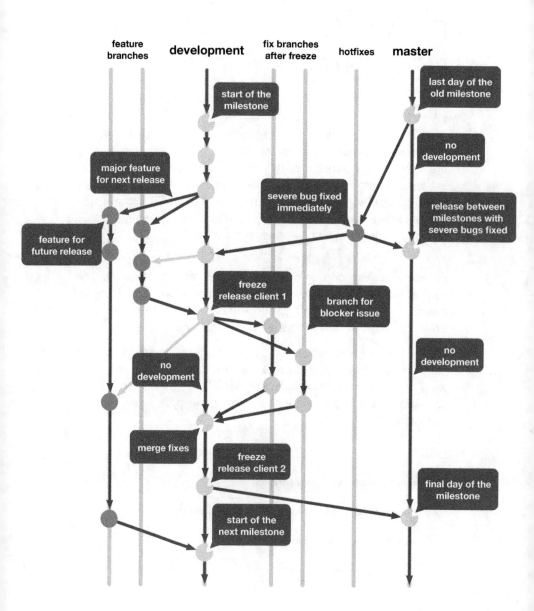

feature branches · development · fix branches after freeze · hotfixes · master

start of the milestone

last day of the old milestone

no development

major feature for next release

severe bug fixed immediately

release between milestones with severe bugs fixed

feature for future release

freeze release client 1

branch for blocker issue

no development

no development

merge fixes

freeze release client 2

final day of the milestone

start of the next milestone

# Master and development

The central *origin* repository holds two branches that will exist for the lifetime of the project:

– master

– development

The *origin/master* branch is similar to the trunk in Subversion. The source code at the *HEAD* (latest commit in the branch) of the master branch points always to a *production* state of the project. The *origin/master* reflects a clean and stable release.

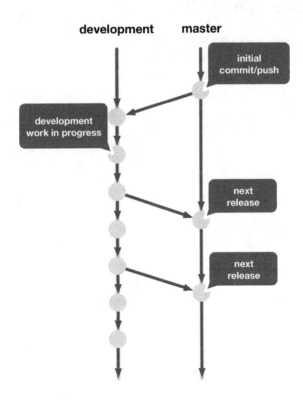

The *origin/development* branch is the main branch for development. Its *HEAD* points to the latest push of the developers. Any automatically triggered build from our continuous integration infrastructure uses this branch. If the project is ready to be released in the release week, the development branch is merged back to the master branch. The master branch is then tagged with the new release number (more on this topic below). Therefore, a merge into the master branch always means that a new production release can and should be made.

There are several cases where branches other than master and development are created. Those cases are explained below.

# Feature branches

**Normally branches off from:** development
**Must merge back into:** development
**Branch naming convention:** issue number or feature name

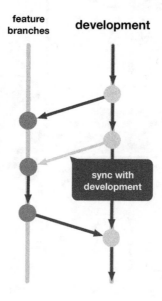

We highly encourage developers to integrate often and to work on the development branch only. But, if it is unknown whether the feature will make it into to the next scheduled release or not, a feature branch should be used. In all other cases developers shouldn't use feature branches. It is up to the developer to keep her branch in sync with the development branch and push it to origin so that its commits are available for other developers. However, if no one else needs the commits the feature branch should not be pushed to origin.

# Example of a feature branch

## Creating a feature branch

When creating a feature branch, the development branch is the start point. A sensible name (e.g., the feature name or the issue number) should be used to create the branch:

```
$ git checkout -b <feature name> development
```

## Syncing the feature branch

The latest commits in the development branch can be merged into the feature branch by:

```
$ git checkout development
$ git pull
$ git checkout <feature name>
$ git merge development
```

## Merging the feature branch back

After finishing the work on the feature branch, it is merged back into the development branch:

```
$ git checkout development
$ git pull
```

```
$ git merge --no-ff <feature name>
$ git push
```

The *--no-ff* flag should always be used to force a merge commit even if the merge can be fast-forwarded.

After merging, the feature branch can be deleted:

```
$ git branch -d <feature name>
```

If the feature branch was pushed to origin, it has to be deleted there as well:

```
$ git push origin :<feature name>
```

# Fix Branches

**Must branch off from:** development after freeze
**Must merge back into:** development
**Branch naming convention:** issue number

These branches are created during the release week after the freeze. A fix branch has to be created for each issue that is fixed during the release week. In comparison to the feature branch, the fix branch has to be pushed to origin so that it can be reviewed. The issue number has to be used as the name of the fix branch and it has to be created from the freezed development branch. Once the change is reviewed, the fix branch is merged back into the development branch and the corresponding issue is marked as reviewed.

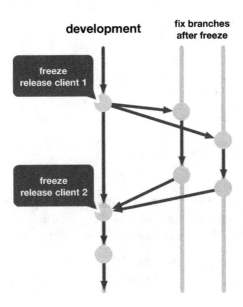

development   fix branches after freeze

freeze
release client 1

freeze
release client 2

## Example of a fix branch
### Creating a fix branch

```
$ git checkout -b <issue number> development
```

### Finishing fix branches

If the work on the issue is done, the fix branches has to be pushed to origin. The *-u* flag has to be used to track the branch.

```
$ git push -u origin <issue number>
```

## Merging fix branches back

After an issue for the next release candidate has been reviewed, the developer who fixed the issue will merge the fix branch back into the development branch:

```
$ git checkout development
$ git pull
$ git merge <issue number>
$ git push
```

It is up to the team lead (or product manager) whether the fix branches are deleted now or after verification. However, they have to be deleted before the next milestone starts:

```
$ git branch -d <issue number>
$ git push origin :<issue number>
```

Since the fix branch was pushed to origin, it has to be deleted remotely, too.

After all fix branches have been merged to the development branch, the next release candidate is created from the development:

```
$ git tag <release candidate 2>
$ git push --tags
```

# Hotfix Branches

**Must branch off from:** master
**Must merge back into:** master and development
**Branch naming convention:** issue number

In case a blocker on the production system has to be fixed and cannot wait for the next regular release, a hotfix branch has to be created from the master branch. Once the hotfix changes are re-viewed, they are merged both into the master and development branches. Then the fixed bug will be released in a small release between milestones.

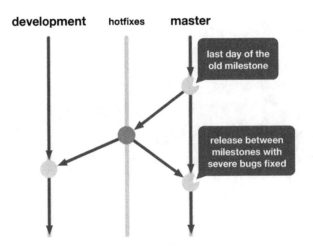

# Example of a hotfix branch
## Creating a hotfix branch

```
$ git checkout -b <issue number> master
# increasing the build version, commit, and push
# fix the blocker
```

## Merging the hotfix branch back

After the blocker has been fixed, reviewed, and verified, the team lead has to merge back the hotfix branch into the master and development branches. Since a minor release will result, a corresponding tag on the master branch has to be made, too:

```
$ git checkout master
$ git merge --no-ff <issue number>
$ git push
$ git tag <release tag>
$ git push --tags
$ git checkout development
$ git pull
$ git merge --no-ff <issue number>
$ git push
```

The hotfix branch can now be deleted

```
$ git branch -d <issue number>
$ git push origin :<issue number>
```

# How to track time

Time tracking is important for controlling purposes and helps keep projects on track and the work load manageable for the team. At Comerge, we track time because of the following reasons:

1.  It serves as a control for the employees to make sure that they have a healthy work–life balance.

2.  It serves as a control for Comerge to ensure that their employees put in their regular hours.

3.  It serves as a basis to analyze if employees working on several projects are able to spend a designated and planned amount of time for the respective projects.

4.  It serves as a basis to control the estimations of work and further improve them for providing correct offers to customers.

5.  It serves as a basis to bill customers.

This leads to the following basic rules:

## Track all the time that is spent working

The first task of an employee entering the office in the morning is to turn on time tracking. Also activities like reading and answering mails, reading up on anything needed for work should be time tracked. It does not include checking facebook (unless it is done for the company's or a customer's sake) or reading newspapers.

## Track the time in the correct project

Make sure that the time is tracked in the correct project. At Comerge, we provide time tracking projects for every internal and external project, sometimes further divided into subprojects for every component. If working on an issue (for example, implementing a feature in the Mobility Android App) this should be tracked in the corresponding time tracking project (e.g., "Mobility.Mobidroid"). Additionally, we have a general purpose project (called "Comerge" in our time tracker) and use it for the time tracking of all tasks that cannot be clearly attributed to a specific project such as reading emails, cleaning up the desk, etc. Scrum meetings, core meetings and tech talks can also be tracked in this project.

## Generally, when working on an issue, track the time on issue basis. Always include the issue number and title

When working on an issue, the general template to use for the time tracking entry is "<project short hand>-<issue number> <issue title>", e.g., "COPILOT-136 Move certain chapters to the CWW". The team lead might request additional information relevant to the issue in the time tracking entry.

## Use meaningful descriptions for tasks without an issue

In general, there should always be an issue and thus the work can be tracked as described in the previous rule. But if, for various reasons, it does not make sense to create an issue (either because creating the issue will take longer than doing the work or the issue can never be closed because it is a frequently recurring task), it is important to use a meaningful description in the time entry. Entering a description saying "Working" does not provide any information. Try to be more specific, e.g., "Triaging incoming issues".

## Team leads or the product manager control the time tracking and provide instructions on how to do it

The product manager or team lead might decide to add additional requirements. He/she may also decide that tracking on issue basis is too fine grained and propose another solution (e.g., tracking development time by writing "Working on issues for milestone 3", because they are not interested in the work time per issue).

## The time tracking entries could be used in retrospective meetings

The comparison of estimated/offered time with the actual time worked on a project or a specific feature helps control the health of a project. We have integrated such a comparison into the retrospective meeting. Since this comparison is presented by the team lead of a component, it is in the interest of the team leads to make sure that their team members track the time correctly.

**If there are any questions on how to track time, the team lead or the product manager should help clarify them.**

# Meetings

# How to hold a meeting

Similar to other creative processes, software development is a collaborative practice and efficient communication with other members of the development team is a key to success. In particular in heterogeneous teams with varying degrees of efficiency, it is important to structure the time spent together—for example in meetings—in an efficient and well organized way. Here are a few hints for preparing a meeting:

## Before the meeting

### Write agenda

The organizer of the meeting prepares a short agenda. This puts all participants in the picture of what will be the content of the meeting and will help them to prepare themselves. The agenda contains ordered topics, including their priority and expected time frame and the agenda tells everybody how they should prepare for the meeting.

### Send agenda to all participants

An agenda on a hidden page is useless. To be effective the organizer needs to send a readable form of the agenda by mail (the agenda directly or a link to the agenda). If a participant has a change request, he will need to announce it to everybody in due time (at least one day ahead) and update the agenda.

## Organize meeting

The organizer appoints a person to record the meeting minutes in advance and informs him. Additionally, he may consider the following questions: Are the necessary tools for the keeper of the minutes available (paper, access to a computer)? Are there comments on the minutes of the previous meeting? Are there any last minute changes to the agenda?

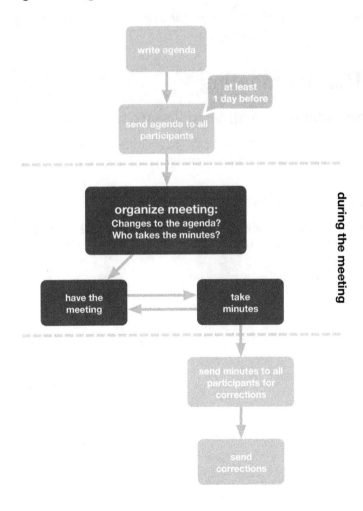

# During the meeting

To make it possible to cover the entire agenda within a reasonable time frame, it is important to stick to the agenda and avoid digressions.

## Write minutes

The keeper of the minutes records the discussion topics, decisions, and any other points of interest.

# After the meeting

## Send minutes to all participants for corrections

After the meeting, the keeper of the minutes sends the meeting minutes to all participants for review.

## Correct minutes

The participants check the minutes for completeness and errors, and send corrections back to the author of the minutes.

# How to hold a Scrum meeting

The goal of the Scrum meeting is to engage all team members, hear about their current advances and visualize the current progress of the project. It is a meeting to see the day-to-day planning of all team members. It takes place every morning and should not last more than 10 minutes. The Scrum meeting relies on the use of a task board containing a grid with one row per team member and the three columns "to do", "in progress", and "done".

## Prepare

The team members prepare the issues that they will be working on during the day in a form suitable for the task board, e.g., a post-it note with issue number and short description of the issue, which can be pinned to the task board.

## Announce

The product manager ensures that the Scrum meeting is held every day; she will make sure that everybody joins the meeting.

## Meet

All team members meet in front of the task board.

## Report

Each team member reports what she did the day before and what she will work on during the day. During this reporting, she moves the issues that she resolved yesterday from "to do" or "in progress" to "done" and adds new issues to the task board in the "to do" and "in progress" columns. Additionally there is a part on the task board that is called the "Backlog". If an issue cannot be completed, it can be moved into this section of the task board. This may happen, for example, because it relies on a component or service that is not yet ready, or because a more urgent issue has come up and overrules all others.

# Common pitfalls

**Granularity of issues:** The amount of work that is needed to complete an issue should not exceed the regular time frame (e.g., more than a day needed to close the issue). Otherwise, it can be frustrating for a team member, because no progress is visible on the task board.

**Too many things on one issue:** There should be only one bug per issue or one feature/enhancement per issue.

The issues for the day are discussed.

**Gossip/chatter:** The meeting leader should avoid letting the discussion run off topic. He also reminds the team members to keep their description of yesterday's work concise.

**Being unclear/mumbling:** The most important point when the team members describe their pending and closed issues is their use of simple words and concise language. Their notes need to be written legibly and they should speak loudly and clearly, such that all participants can follow their presentation.

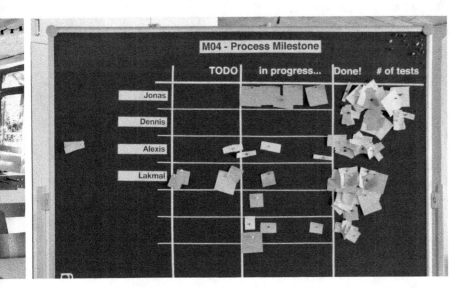

A typical Scrum board.

# How to participate in a core meeting

Despite all the sophisticated tools and communication channels, software development can feel like a solitary exercise. Developers go to the office in the morning, get connected to the network and start developing the code of their component. Often they achieve the best results when they get into a flow and quit noticing the world around them. The core meeting (at Comerge, we hold it on Friday afternoon) is an institution that gives everybody an opportunity to show what he or she did in the past week and to demonstrate it to the others. The core meeting is an important part of our company culture and we found core meetings to be efficient up to 15 participants.

## Prepare

In the morning before the weekly core meeting, all participants should prepare what they plan to say during the meeting. They may produce notes to help present a report and prevent forgetting any key aspects. Also, if a team member plans a demo, she should test it before (best: test it on the presentation machine).

## Be there on time

As all company members participate in the core meeting, delays result in a waste of time with a high multiplier. The organizer should make sure that all participants know when the meeting is scheduled and all participants should appear in time for the meeting.

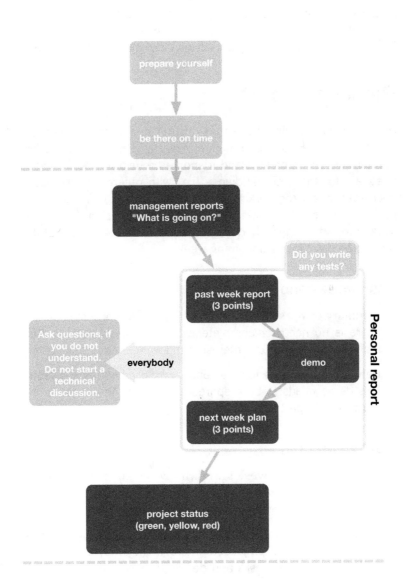

# Management report

At the beginning of the meeting, the management gives a statement on general information and announcements. The management also reports on strategic decisions and plans for the future.

# Personal report

In turn, every participant gives a short personal report. The report should contain enough information to put all others in the picture of their current progresses and it should be held in a form that is adequate for the entire audience (i.e., with different professional backgrounds and/or working on different projects). The personal report comprises two main aspects of every participant's current work: a report on the work done in the past week and a plan of the work to be done in the upcoming week.

## Past week report

- **Summary of work:** Describes the three most important points. There is no need for completeness, an overview suffices. The main goal is to produce interest in the work.

- **Demo:** Whenever possible, the report should include a short demo. This demo needs to be prepared and tested. The demo is the most exciting part of the core meeting.

## Next week plan

- **Description of next week's work:** Provides an idea of planned activities for the next week. Again, three main points are sufficient, no need for completeness.

- **Questions:** The core meeting is a chance for the participants working on different projects to interact. They may find similarities in their current tasks and decide to have a deeper technical discussion off line. Questions may be asked during the core meeting, but they should stay focused and mainly target clarifications. In-depth discussion should be taken off line.

# Team lead status report

Every team lead has to summarize the status of his current project, using the following scale:

- **Green:** Everything is fine, the project is going well.

- **Yellow:** The project is going as planned, but there are some problems or uncertainties that need to be resolved. Yellow means that a team lead wants to talk to the product manager or the company's management about the state of the project.

- **Red:** The project is definitely not going as planned, problems have to be fixed. Management needs to help/act.

# How to hold a retrospective meeting

As stated in the introduction, everything we describe here is subject to evolution and we constantly try to improve the processes of the Co-Pilot. To learn from mistakes, they must be identified and actions developed to counter their repetition. This is the goal of the retrospective meeting.

## Goal

In the retrospective meeting the team discusses their perception of the completed milestone. The retrospective meeting acts as an open discussion platform. If the team identifies a problem, they discuss countermeasures as part of the processes to prevent it from reoccurring.

## Before

### Product manager invites to the meeting

There is no special need for an extensive agenda. Instead, the product manager should create a wiki page based on the retrospective meeting template. The mail to the participants should include a link to this page, with a request to add positive and negative points before the meeting.

*How to hold a retrospective meeting*

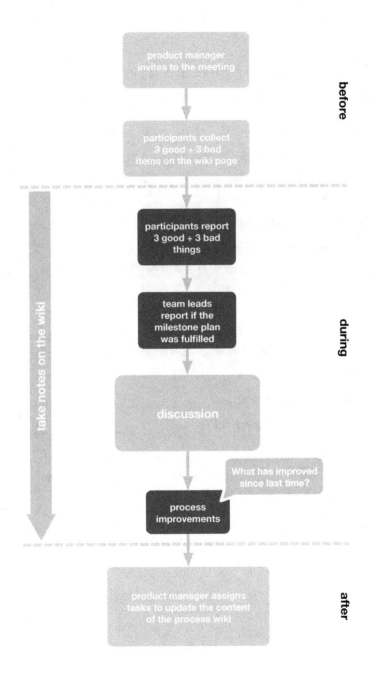

75

# During

## Three positive and three negative points

Each participant writes three positive and three negative points about the milestone on the wiki meeting page in advance. Participant reports: Every participant gives an explanation on

- three items that went well during the milestone.

- three items that went badly during the milestone.

## Milestone plan validation

Each team lead reports if the milestone plan was fulfilled for his component, and if not, why they failed to do so.

## Discussion

Each point of the above will be discussed and new possible improvements to the process are suggested.

- What needs to be changed?

- How should it be changed?

- How will the improvements be tested?

The participants also discuss any open issues and countermeasures that arose in past retrospective meetings. If the process was improved by addressing an issue through a countermeasure and succeeded in an improvement, the issue is closed. If the problem persists, it will be added to the discussion list again. The meeting leader adds all discussed points to the wiki meeting page.

# After

## Assigning tasks

The product manager creates issues on the process issue tracker to add these improvements to the process and assigns them to her members.

# Tests

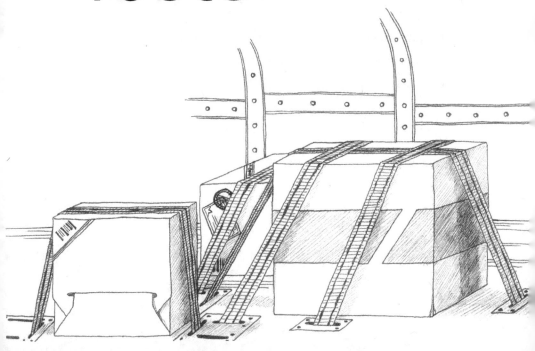

# How to test

Testing is a fundamental part of the software development process. At Comerge, we view testing as a continuous process that is tightly integrated into our daily work through the following rules:

1. Never release without testing.

2. Never change code without unit tests (if a unit test can be developed).

3. Never implement a new feature without a unit test infrastructure to test the new feature.

Testing comes in various flavors that complement each other. Using all of them in combination ensures a high quality end product. The following test strategies exist:

- **Unit test:** Automatic tests executed by an automatic build system.

- **Smoke test:** A test document executed by a tester.

- **Release test:** Free style testing executed by a group of testers driven by a test plan.

- **Acceptance test:** End users working with the product.

# A sample test plan

A test plan contains instructions on how to test all the new features and all the issues that were implemented and fixed during the iteration. The test plan assigns testers to certain features that should be tested. If in a later step a regression is found, the tester can be contacted to find out whether it already existed at this step.

| | Benno | Michela | Eva | Sara | Till |
|---|---|---|---|---|---|
| **Comerge Process grammar and content** | | | | | |
| **Grammatical correction (Eva, Till – Questions: Michela)** The chapters have been printed out and are now on the desks of the testers who need to read them. Please read them through thoroughly and check for any formal or grammatical mistakes. For formal mistakes, please refer to the guidelines in issues COPILOT-173 and COPILOT-178. | | | | | |
| **Check if all occurrences of Origo have been replaced with JIRA (Benno, Michela – Questions: Eva)** Our old issue tracking system Origo has been replaced with JIRA. There should not be any occurrences of Origo in the Process. Please check the chapters online in the wiki for that. | | | | | |
| **All non-canon Process chapters should have been moved to the CWW wiki (Michela, Sara – Questions: Eva)** We have removed a few chapters from the Process this time around. They are now in the CWW. You can access them from the CWW main page. Please check that the following chapters have been moved: - How to apply for holidays - How to manage and plan an event - How to give a presentation - How to sell - How to do personal education/training - How to create a good design - How to interview job candidates | | | | | |
| **Comerge Process layout tests** | | | | | |
| **Ensure readability (Sara, Till – Questions: Eva)** The main body text has a different typeface. Read it for a while and try to see if it is comfortable for the eye. | | | | | |
| **The dust jacket (Benno, Michela - Questions: Eva)** The Comerge Process book now has a dust jacket. It has to be checked for grammar mistakes as well as design mistakes. Do all the graphics look ok or are there for example - lines that overlap? - things that are not well aligned? - etc. | | | | | |

# How to unit test

Whenever a software developer implements a new enhancement or fixes a bug, the developed code should be accompanied by a unit test. As a consequence, the test suite will grow together with the system's source code base. The key goal of unit testing is to prevent regressions. Providing a well designed test case (or a set of test cases) for a particular issue together with its implementation will ensure that future breaking changes to the code will be detected if the test suite is run regularly. Of course, the quality of the test suite determines its ability to detect breaking changes. How to write good tests is an art by itself and goes beyond the scope of this process documentation. The process for resolving an issue and developing the associated unit test follows the scheme described below.

## Take a bug or an enhancement

As a first step, the software developer decides on an issue to resolve. This may be a bug or an enhancement.

## Write a unit test

Before actually implementing the fix or feature, she writes a unit test testing the changes. This is called test driven development. Writing unit tests before developing the source code to resolve an issue ensures the following key points:

- The developer actually writes unit tests.

- Without the code the unit tests fail and hence, unnecessary developments do not occur.

- The design of the code makes it possible to write unit tests.

## Implement issue

In a third step, she develops the fix for the bug or implementation of the feature.

## Commit

Once the unit tests pass locally, she commits her code.

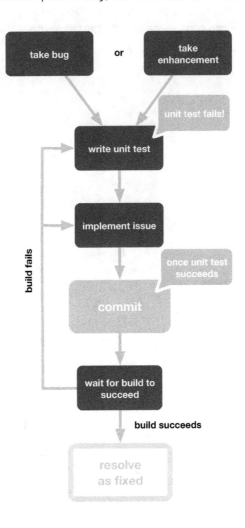

## Wait for build to succeed

After the commit, an automatic build will run. If the build succeeds, the issue is considered as resolved. If the build fails, further improvements are necessary.

## Resolve as fixed

In a last step, the issue's state is set to fixed and the issue can be closed. The source code has been integrated in the software system and tested.

# How to smoke test

The goal of smoke testing is to find blocking issues before the customers or end users receive a build. The team lead appoints a smoke tester. The smoke tester is a team member. The smoke tester uses the smoke test document to test a given build. The smoke test document describes tests for all important features of the software and hence, ensures the correct execution and usability of those features. The following sequence of steps, help carry out a smoke test:

## Take build

A smoke test requires a software build as testing object. A smoke test may test any kind of build, but most commonly it is done once a week to verify an integration build.

## Smoke test

The smoke tester takes the smoke test document and tests the build. The smoke test is usually considered successful, if no blocking bug was discovered. Otherwise, the developing team needs to fix the found bugs and repeat the smoke test with a new build. For a definition of severities, see **How to work with issues**.

If a software runs on several different OS versions or as a web application on several different browsers, the smoke test has to be performed at least on the most important OS and the most important browsers the software is running on to ensure quality.

# Fix bugs

If the smoke tester discovers a blocker bug, it needs to be fixed immediately and a new build is produced after the fix.

A smoke test document contains stories describing how the smoke tester should use the software and what he should be able to achieve. Typically, smoke test documents grow over time to become long documents that cover most of the core features of the software. Writing smoke test documents also helps evaluate whether the software is easy to understand.

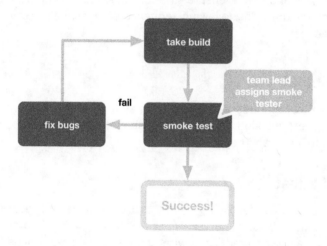

# How to test a release

The goal of release testing is to ensure the high quality of new and existing features. Testing a release may take up to several days, but usually one day is enough. During these days, the source code is only changed if a blocking issue prevents testing. A smoke test before release testing minimizes the likelihood of having a blocking issue in the release candidate.

## Setup release candidate

The release testers need access to a release candidate. For example, they may need to download and install a release candidate on their local machine.

## Choose test item from test plan

Every tester has a set of test items assigned to him. He chooses in which order he will test them, but the final goal is to cover all assigned test items. In a first step, he chooses one of the test items.

## Test the test item

He tests the item by following the test item description. The main goal is to make the new feature fail and/or to find usability issues. The tester creates a new issue report for each problem he discovers.

## Mark tested items on test plan

After having worked through a test item, the tester marks the item as tested on the test plan. At Comerge, we print the test plan, pin it to a wall, and all testers mark what they have tested on this sheet. He then goes to the first step again and tests the next item until none of his items are untested any more.

## Ensure all items tested

The product manager ensures that all items from the test plan have been tested. To do so, she checks whether the testers have marked all assigned test items as "done" on the test plan.

## Improve smoke test document

Some test items from the test plan can become part of the smoke test document. The team lead assigns a team member responsible for updating the smoke test document.

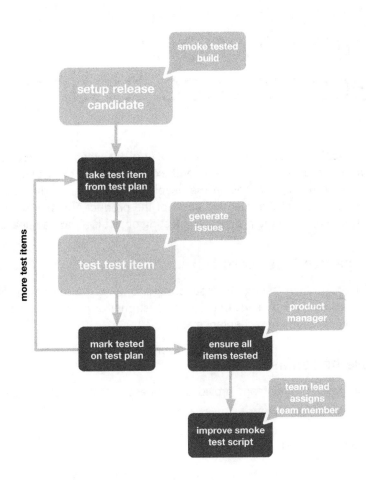

# How to do acceptance testing

The goal of acceptance testing is to find out whether a product fulfills the users' requirements and expectations. In particular, acceptance testing focuses on the usability of the final product and makes sure that the intended users of the product are able to efficiently work with the product. The testing object is always a release.

## Organize test users

For acceptance testing, the testers need to be part of the group of the product's end users. Usually, the customer organizes the availability of testers for acceptance tests.

## Create release

The development team provides a release as testing object. See How to create a release.

## Instruct test users

It is unlikely that the testers of an acceptance test have worked with the product before. Thus, they need clear instructions on several properties of the product and the testing procedure, covering

- what they can expect from the software

- what they cannot expect from the software

- how they should carry out the tests

- what they should test

- how they can provide feedback

## Let test users test release

The acceptance testing duration may be set to several days. During this time, the testers may individually test the software.

## Collect and process feedback

The most important step in the acceptance testing process is to collect as much feedback as possible from the testers. The development team then creates issues based on the testers' feedback.

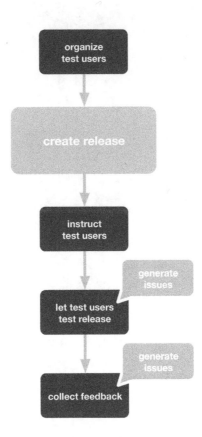

# Customers

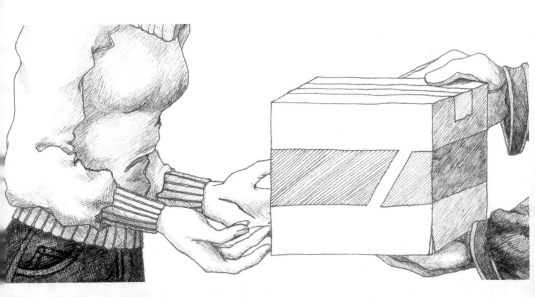

# How to work with customers

Many customers are not familiar with the methodology of agile software development and are, in consequence, often surprised by the extent of their involvement that is expected of them during the development phase. Constant exchange and communication are, however, a key factor for progressing in the desired direction even if voids in specifications are discovered or if requirements are changed or extended. The following sections list a number of proven measures for handling relationships with customers and for functional communication interfaces:

## Infrastructure for communication with the customer

A shared issue tracking platform provides an effective means for organizing work packages, filing bugs and feature requests and allows to document decisions and store documents in a relevant way. It is important to reach a common understanding on how to use this platform. Again, many customers are not familiar with using such a platform as primary form for written communication.

The use of a shared calendar helps organize meetings, synchronize project deadlines, and provides information on the availability of the involved parties (e.g., holidays).

Discussions are most efficiently conducted by talking to each other, so favor phone calls or face-to-face meetings over writing emails.

## Understanding the customer

Understanding the job and the ideas of the customer in its entirety is a precondition for successful project completion. Exposing the development team as much as possible to the customer's business, for example by organizing visits to the customer, may help to identify how software can improve the processes of the customer. The clearer the business is to the development team, the better the end product will fit the customer's needs.

Another way to develop an understanding for the needs and ideas of the customer is to ask him for stories describing what he seeks to accomplish with the software.

When customers do software testing, it is important to acknowledge that they typically are not professional testers. The understanding that finding issues is good, not bad, does not come naturally and should be emphasized. Support the customer in filing issues that are meaningful to the development team.

The answer to a customer request or a decision should never be "this won't work". Instead, the line of argumentation should show consequences of decisions. Consequences can always be found in the triangle: time, costs and functionality (or quality) and can help the customer to understand the implications of a decision.

## Bases for discussions with the customer

The product manager holds a weekly conference call (during critical phases also more often) with the project leaders of the customer. Additional participants can be invited when this makes sense. All participants prepare discussion points, ideally by means of an agenda that is distributed beforehand. Decisions can be taken immediately and should be documented in the form of issues and possibly meeting minutes.

A monthly controlling meeting with the people in charge at the customer serves to inform them and to market the project.

# How to do customer support

Contracts with customers may not only involve software, but also software services. After a product is released and used productively by the customer, support questions and/or situations may arise. This page serves as a guide for planning and providing such support services.

**Infrastructure:** All projects requiring/offering support to customers must address the following issues:

- Separation of support tiers ("1$^{st}$/2$^{nd}$ level support").

- Timetable to cover support timespan and responsibilities.

- Email infrastructure: Often, the customer will use other communication channels to report an incident or seek support than we do, for example because he uses another system internally. An automated email system serves as an interface between customers seeking support, support staff, and management (for bookkeeping/invoicing).

## Example tiers

This example explains the tier setup between Comerge and a fictional company "Initech". It illustrates the notion of support tiers and describes a possible setup.

### 1$^{st}$ level

Employees of Initech at their office in Geneva provide 1$^{st}$ level support to all connected stakeholders, i.e., traders and/or management of affiliated banks.

- 1st level support is the main interface for stakeholders, all support requests are channeled through it.

- When initializing any support activity, a ticket is opened. This serves to track progress, findings, communication, and time (e.g., for bookkeeping data) for all parties.

- 1st level support acts directly on all support requests that can be processed given their tools, specifically

  - General questions

  - Actions involving the back-end rich client

- Actions requiring further assistance are escalated to 2nd level support using the support tickets, e.g., directly changing database values, etc.

- The telephone hotline at Comerge serves as a red phone for urgent assistance requiring immediate actions.

## 2nd level

Comerge provides 2nd level support for Initech.

- It reacts on incoming support tickets within reasonable time depending on their priority. Support tickets may be answered/ acted on outside of the hotline hours.

- Comerge provides telephone support for urgent problems. This hotline is guaranteed to be active during the arranged hours.

- 2nd level support has full access to all systems, and therefore handles any problems requiring direct manipulation of these systems' software, i.e., all applications belonging to the Initech system.

# Glossary

# Glossary

## A

**Acceptance test:** *Acceptance tests* are done by the people who are part of the final end user group of the product.

**Assigned issue:** An *issue* can be assigned to a *team member*. Such an issue is called an assigned issue. If the *issue* is assigned to a *team member* it is expected, that the assignee resolves the *issue*. Only an assigned and planned *issue* can be fixed.

## B

**Build:** The result of *building*. There are a number of different kind of builds:

- **Continuous build:** A build which runs "all the time". Usually, such a build is automatically triggered whenever the build machine detects a code change. This build is tested by *unit tests* only.

- **Integration build:** A build which integrates code changes from multiple *teams*. Usually, takes place once a week and is tested by *unit tests* and *smoke tests*.

- **Milestone build:** The build which results from a *milestone*. Usually, takes place every 5 weeks and is tested *unit tests*, *smoke tests*, and *release tests*.

**Building:** The process of converting source code files into stand-alone software artifacts that can be run on a computer.

**Blocker:** An *issue* with *severity* blocker. See *severity* for details.

# C

**Critical issue:** An *issue* which has at least a *severity* of critical. See *severity* for details.

**Code owner:** The developer who is responsible for a portion of the source code. Frequently, the code owner is the developer who wrote the code in the first place. But over time, the ownership of code can change. The code owner is responsible to maintain the owned code. The code owner is also the expert for the owned code. It is considered a violation of the *netiquette* if someone changes code he/she does not own without approval of the code owner.

**Component:** One part of a *product*. Usually, a *team* owns several components. The component owner is responsible for maintaining the component. Splitting a product into components such that the components can be developed in parallel by several teams is difficult. It is common practice to split a product at least into a core and a UI component. The core component provides the model (data) and the UI component provides a user interface, which allows to present and modify the model.

**Continuous build:** One type of a *build*. See *build* for details.

**Customer:** A *customer* is a *process role*.

# D

**Decompression phase:** The time after a *release* in which the pressure on the *team members* is minimized to give them time to recover and spend time on things with low priority.

**Duplicate issue:** An *issue* which is a duplicate of another *issue*. This means that the exact same *issue* was reported before. Such *issues* are *resolved* as duplicate.

**Door opener:** A person you interact with during the sales process. In oder to be able to talk to a potential buyer, you need to get to them.

A door opener is a person from your network who introduces you to the potential buyer or at least can help you to get a meeting with them.

## F

**Filed against:** An *issue* can be filed against a *team*. This means, that the *issue* is owned by the *team* and the owning *team* is responsible to either resolve the *issue* or file it against another *team*. The *team* owning the code causing the *issue* should own the *issue* in the end.

**Fix day:** A day during which only *bugs* are fixed.

**Feature:** A feature is a function of the software to be created. All features together constitute the *product*.

## G

**Gatekeeper:** A person who controls access to a resource you wish to acquire or a person you wish to interact with. In the sales process, a gatekeeper typically stands in the way between you and a potential buyer you want to contact.

## I

**Integration build:** One type of a *build*. See *build* for details.

**Inbox:** All *issues* with state *new* are considered to be part of the inbox. Besides the global inbox each *component* also has an inbox. A *new issue* can be assigned to a *component* to become part of the assigned *component*'s inbox.

**Inbox triager:** The one responsible to triage *issues* from a *component*'s inbox. See **How to triage issues** for details.

**Issue:** Something to do. It is either a *bug* to fix, or an *enhancement* to implement. An *issue* has an *issue state*, a *severity* and a *priority*.

**Issue owner:** The owner of an *issue*. It is the one which is *assigned* to the *issue*. See also *assigned issue*.

**Issue report:** The report of an *issue*. Usually *issues* are reported in written form using an *issue tracker*.

**Issue state:** An *issue* has exactly one state. For a list of all possible states refer to How to work with issues.

**Issue tracker:** A software which can be used to report and track *issues*. Well known *issue tracker* systems are bugzilla, Trac, JIRA, and Origo.

**Issue triage:** Triage means to take something and put it into the correct place, where it belongs. For an *issue* this means that the *issue* is either resolved and/or assigned to a *team* and/or a *target*. See How to triage issues for details.

**Iteration:** One cycle in the release process. Usually an *iteration* is 5 weeks long. Each *iteration* has 3 phases:

- **Planning:** 2–3 Days

- **Implementing:** ~4 weeks

- **Testing:** 1 week, see How to plan a project for details.

# M

**Milestone:** A *milestone* either refers to an *iteration* or to a *milestone build* depending on the context.

**Milestone build:** See *builds*.

# N

**Netiquette:** Implicit rules within a project/process culture which every participant should follow. A violation of the netiquette might be considered an offense by other participants. Following is an incomplete list of things not to do:

- Do not change code you don't own.

- Do not commit code which does not compile.

- Do not bypass the *team lead*.

- Do not close *issues* as *won't fix* unless you have a really good reason to do so.

**New and Noteworthy:** A document, usually a web page, describing all the new and noteworthy *features* of a release of a product. The idea is to give your users a quick overview of what could be of interest to them.

# P

**Planned issue:** An *issue* assigned to a *release* is considered a *planned issue*. If the *issue* is assigned to a *release*, it is expected that the *issue* is fixed within the assigned *release*. Only *issues* which are planned and assigned can be fixed.

**Priority:** An *issue* can have a *priority* assigned. See **How to work with issues** for details about priorities.

**Product:** The software to be created. The sum of all *features*.

**Product release:** The final *release*.

**Product manager:** A *product manager* is a *process role*.

**Process:** Activities or tasks that produce a specific service or product for a *customer*. The *process* describes how the entities which participate in a *project* cooperate to create one or several *products*.

**Process role:** Different roles within a process, see **Process roles**.

**Project:** The goal of a *project* is to create one or several *products* using a *process*.

# R

**Regression:** If a code change introduces a new *bug* this *bug* is called a *regression*. Something which used to work is now broken.

**Release:** A tested *build*. The result of an *iteration*.

**Release candidate:** A possible *release*. The *release candidate* is tested to decide if it has the quality to qualify as a *release*. See How to create a release for details.

**Release test:** *Release testing* happens during the release week, before the product is given to the customers for *acceptance testing*. Its goal is to ensure a high release candidate quality.

**Reopen issue:** The *process* of changing a fixed *issue*'s *state* back to *triaged* or *opened*.

**Reporter:** The one who reported an *issue*.

**Requirement:** Something which is required for a *product* to make a *release*. The *product manager* is responsible in identifying this requirement together with the *customer*.

**Resolve issue:** The *process* of changing the *state* of an issue to *resolved*.

**Resolved:** A state of an *issue*. See *issue* for details.

**Resolution:** Several different causes can change the state of an *issue* to the final states *resolved*, *closed*, or *verified*. See How to work with issues for a list of all the possible resolutions.

**Review:** A code change is checked by a programmer other than the one who wrote the code change. Usually, this peer review happens before the code change is released into the source repository. The goal of a review is that the released code has high quality and does not introduce a *regression*.

**Role:** See *process role*.

# S

**Severity:** A *bug* can have different levels of *severities*. An *enhancement* has no *severity*, but a *priority*. See **How to work with issues** for details about *severities*.

**Signing off a build:** The *team leads* and the *product manager* can sign off a *build*. If everybody has signed off the *build*, it is released and the next *iteration* starts.

**Smoke test:** A *smoke test* is done before a build is given to a customer for more extensive testing and has the purpose of making sure that it will not catastrophically fail. Often *smoke tests* are manual executions of the most important operations. For example, in a reservation system this would include creating, editing, and canceling reservations.

**Stakeholder:** Everyone interested in a *product*: *team member*, *team lead*, *product manager*, *customer*.

# T

**Team:** A set of *team members*. Every *team* has a *team lead*.

**Team lead:** A *team lead* is a *process role*.

**Team leader:** See *team lead*.

**Team member:** A *team member* is a *process role*.

**Test day:** During the test day a *release candidate* is tested. No code is changed unless it is required to resolve a *blocker*.

**Test plan:** The test plan contains at least who tests what on which system. For example: Benno tests edit image on Firefox 3.5. See **How to test** for more details.

# U

**Unit test:** A *unit test* checks an individual unit of the source code using test data to find out if it is fit for use. A unit can be single methods or an interface. *Unit tests* should always be independent from other *unit tests*, so that they can be run individually, in parallel, or in sequence.

**User:** The one using the *product*.

**User error:** A mistake made by a *user* which might look like an *issue* at first glance. Such *issues*, if reported, are usually resolved as *works for me*.

# V

**Verified:** An *issue* state and *resolution*. See *issue* for details.

**Verify issue:** The *process* of changing the state of an *issue* to *verified*. The verifier tries to reproduce the *issue* – if he cannot, the *issue* is considered verified.

**Verify fix:** The same as *verify issue*.

# W

**Won't fix:** An *issue* which will not be fixed. It is one of the *resolution* states of an *issue*.

**Works for me:** An *issue* that can not be reproduced.